Advanced Dungeons & Dragons Adventure 5

Eye of Pain

by Thomas M. Reid

Table of Contents

Credits

Editing: Miranda Horner
Creative Director: Steve Winter
Cover Illustration: Dana Knutson
Interior Illustrations: Arnie Swekel
Cartography: Roy Boholst
Typography: Tracey L. Isler
Graphic Design: Shan Ren, Greg Kerkman, and Paul Hanchette
Art Director: Stephen A. Daniele
Playtesting and Advice: Steven Brown, Shaun A. Horner, Cindi Rice, Wayne Rice,
Phil A. Richardson, Keith Strohm, and Alex W. West

TSR, Inc.
201 Sheridan Springs Road
Lake Geneva,
WI 53147
U.S.A.

TSR Ltd.
120 Church End,
Cherry Hinton
Cambridge CB1 3LB
United Kingdom

Introduction

Welcome to *Eye of Pain,* an adventure designed for characters of levels 4 to 8 (for a total of 35 levels) that can be played separately or as the first of a trilogy. The other two adventures in the series are *Eye of Doom* and *Eye to Eye.* As always, before you attempt to run this adventure, you should familiarize yourself with the plot and individual encounters. If you are pressed for time, at the very least skim through the text, noting the main sections, and read only the first two sections (Background and Beginning the Adventure) in any detail.

Eye of Pain is set up so that you can utilize it almost anywhere in your campaign world. The locations are generic enough that they can easily be renamed, if needed, to match a particular region that is already detailed in your setting. Simply pick out a place that is forested and remote enough to allow for the kinds of beasts and other events that are noted herein.

Be aware that although this adventure is designed for mid-level characters, it should not be taken lightly by the players. *Eye of Pain* revolves around some of the more well-known but potentially underrated creatures in the AD&D® game system: the beholder and its kin. This is not just a hack-and-slash affair; characters who venture forth intent on stomping into the beasts' lair and slaying them without any forethought and preparation are in for a nasty surprise. In fact, the PCs will be hard pressed to survive against the cunning machinations of the creatures, much less actually succeed.

Although the DM does not need anything other than the *Dungeon Master® Guide,* the *Player's Handbook,* and the Monstrous Manual™ accessory to get full use out of this adventure, it is part of the Monstrous Arcana™ series of products that includes *I, Tyrant,* a sourcebook on beholders. *I, Tyrant* is a perfect complement to the entire beholder trilogy of adventures, providing the DM with all sorts of additional information on beholders and beholder kin. It can serve as an invaluable method of spicing up the characters' encounters with the nasty creatures in this and the following adventures. In fact, some of the material provided in this work comes from *I, Tyrant.*

Background

Far removed from surface habitations, deep beneath the ground, a cancerous abomination is festering. A hive of beholders has taken root, biding its time until the glorious day when it can rise up and reclaim ancient sacred beholder lands from its hated enemies, the humans. The hive mother, a great, lumbering behemoth known as Ixathinon, rules the hive with an iron grip, demanding the strictest obedience from her minions.

One such subordinate, however, has other ideas and has been carefully implementing its *own* insidious plans, unbeknownst to the hive mother. Qeqtoxii, an elder orb, has kept its true identity a secret from the hive mother by posing as a mere true beholder. It hopes someday to claim leadership of the hive for its own. In order to do this, however, Qeqtoxii must defeat and destroy the hive mother, which is a formidable task, indeed.

Thus, Qeqtoxii has decided to utilize outside forces in its quest for supremacy—namely, unwitting adventurers. As a part of its plans, the elder orb has carefully set up a secret hideaway far from the hive, where it has been spying on a small settlement in the guise of a human, observing activities, gathering information, and luring unsuspecting people to do its bidding. It plans to recruit an adventuring team and then test them by allowing them to invade its secret lair. In this way, Qeqtoxii hopes to learn if the heroes are capable of facing a beholder and destroying it. If they show promise through success, then the elder orb will "allow" them to find additional clues that will lead them back to the hive and the hive mother.

Qeqtoxii plans to lure the player characters into working for it by disguising itself as Velinax the Vermilion, a wizard interested in beholder lore and looking for brave heroes to accompany him into a reputed beholder lair. He has as his partner another wizard named Tarren Traskar. Tarren has been thoroughly taken in by Qeqtoxii and works with the elder orb to convince the characters to join the team.

The heroes will have competition, however.

Qeqtoxii is no fool; it knows better than to test just one group. It has also been recruiting other adventuring groups (disguised as a different individual each time), figuring that one way to determine which of them is best suited to its needs is to put them into head-to-head competition and see who winds up on top.

The characters are convinced by Velinax and Tarren to meet them at Burke's Crossing, a small logging community, but the two wizards never show up, leaving the PCs without any clear idea of what to do next. One other adventuring group does arrive, though, and it becomes clear that they are looking for the beholder lair, too. They are not interested in any kind of alliance, however. Without the two wizards, the PCs have no idea of where to begin resolving the situation, so they must begin their own research.

As the player characters begin to make inquiries, they learn a little about what the community has been experiencing. Recently, the lumberjacks working the forest upriver from Burke's Crossing have made a series of unnerving discoveries. Several months ago, some of the locals began to disappear. Since there was no evidence left behind, tracking the missing people was impossible. Then one night, a statue was left in a clearing in the woods. It was a bust of a man set atop a pedestal. No one knew where the statue had come from or who the figure was. After that, folks would occasionally see movement or lights in the trees near where the statue had been left, but nothing was ever tracked. Now, quite a few of the loggers have left the camp, refusing to work because they believe the forest is haunted.

Of course, the truth of the matter is that Qeqtoxii was merely destroying victims using its *disintegrate* power, and because it levitates, the elder orb left no footprints behind. The statue was simply a traveler, a stranger to these parts, that Qeqtoxii had encountered and petrified. The elder orb had set about carving away portions of the stranger's body until only the bust

Background

was left. Qeqtoxii then fashioned a stone pedestal in the same manner and used *tele-kinesis* to move both pieces into position. All of this activity was purely an effort on the elder orb's part to be spooky and unnerving—the statue serves no other purpose than this.

The player characters may also investigate the whereabouts of the two wizards, Velinax and Tarren. A few careful inquiries reveal that the wizards have a room at the local inn paid up through the end of the month, but they haven't been seen since the morning of the PCs' arrival. If the characters choose to pursue this lead, they eventually discover some notes detailing several reasons why the two wizards suspected that a beholder was nearby, as well as several clues that reveal a possible location for its lair. Of course, all of this is merely planted evidence left by Qeqtoxii for the PCs to find.

Other clues begin to crop up if the PCs take their time tracking down the lair. In addition, other events occur within the little village, including several red herrings designed to throw the players off track. In the end, if the characters haven't figured out that there is a beholder in their midst, Qeqtoxii gives up on them and starts its test over on a different group of heroes, and the adventure is effectively over.

Once the characters do actually try to track down the lair of the beholder, the clues that have been "provided" by Qeqtoxii lead right to the caverns. However, at some point before the characters actually find and enter the caverns, they encounter what they think is the beholder lurking in the trees. In the likely event that they attack it, they quickly discover that it is actually Tarren Traskar. Qeqtoxii had used a *veil* spell to give Tarren the appearance of being a beholder in an effort to lure the characters into his lair. Of course, if they wish to, the PCs can attack the "beholder," but the spell's duration elapses after the first combat round. Tarren attempts to get closer to the party simply because he wishes to get help from the PCs.

Tarren's true form is revealed after the first combat round or after he is slain. If the latter is the case, there is some bit of life still in him, and

he will reveal in his dying breaths that a beholder had cast a spell on him for reasons he can only guess at. Since Tarren is a little disoriented from his ordeal, any answers he gives the PCs are a little vague.

The remainder of the adventure is taken up with the exploration of the beholder's lair. During this part of the adventure, the characters may stumble upon the "remains" of the other party of heroes, who were unsuccessful in their own endeavors to vanquish the beholder hiding there. Ultimately, the PCs must face a death tyrant that was created solely for this purpose by Qeqtoxii. The elder orb itself is nowhere to be found, having left this testing ground through a back escape route the moment the characters arrived. The lair has a generous allotment of traps and tricks, as well as a sprinkling of minions, but once the fight with the death tyrant is over and done with, observant characters should realize that the monster they have just defeated is not the creature that has been wreaking havoc around Burke's Crossing. The trail does not end here.

Beginning the Adventure

The characters should first be contacted by Velinax and Tarren while they are in another community nearby. If you want to run this adventure as an isolated mini-campaign (perhaps tying it in with the other two adventures in the series) then the place is known as Cumbert, a nondescript small town. Beyond that, the details do not matter much; feel free to flesh it out further. If, however, you want to place the adventure into an existing campaign, then choose a community that has appropriate terrain features nearby where you can place Burke's Crossing and the logging camp. Whichever the case, the characters can learn about the occurrences taking place near Burke's Crossing through two different events, detailed below.

The Posting

This event is set up rather loosely in order to allow you to work it into whatever other activities the characters are involved in. Whether they are relaxing in a tavern or inn, working on some other adventure, or perhaps in the service of some noble or government official, they should be able to stumble across a posting board somewhere in Cumbert. If that doesn't fit the atmosphere of your particular campaign, then perhaps they hear the news from a town crier.

Whatever the form of the announcement, the PCs should see (or hear) the following post:

> Notice: Heroes and sellswords needed for research expedition. Some potentially dangerous work hunting monsters, but pay is excellent. Must be willing to work in the presence of magic. For more information, seek out Velinax the Vermilion and Tarren Traskar at the Grumbling Goblin here in Cumbert.

If the characters are not currently involved in any sort of adventure at the moment, then they might very well be at the Grumbling Goblin when they see this notice. If the PCs do not attempt to make contact, then Velinax and Tarren eventually seek them out by using a paid messenger. This will occur at some point while the characters are in Cumbert either relaxing in a tavern,

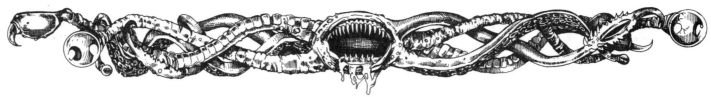

Beginning the Adventure

buying supplies at the local store, or maybe even visiting another employer. If this is the case, read the following aloud to the players:

> A young lad of perhaps 12 or 14 years of age strolls up. He seems to be smirking slightly, as if he knows some secret all the rest of the world does not. He begins speaking to one of you. "Ah, excuse me. I'm supposed to give this to you." He holds out a rolled piece of parchment.

The boy does not leave immediately after delivering the message; he waits around expectantly to be paid for his services, even though Velinax already gave him a considerable amount to deliver the message. If the PCs pay him, he thanks them sincerely and disappears. If they refuse and shoo him away, he leaves, but he has successfully picked the pocket of one of them; either choose or select randomly one small item belonging to one of the characters (a gem is a good choice) to be taken. When that character tries to pull the item out at a later date, inform the player that the item is missing.

When the characters read the parchment, read the following aloud to the players:

> Greetings. You have made something of a name for yourselves recently, and we believe you are well suited to a venture we are planning. If you are interested in hearing more of our business proposition, then please meet us at the Grumbling Goblin for a free round of drinks to discuss it further. We think you might find the offer very promising. Velinax the Vermilion and Tarren Traskar.

If the characters decide to follow up on this message, go to The Meeting.

The Meeting

Once the characters seek out the two wizards at the Grumbling Goblin (whether they are following up on the general posting or the personal message), read the following to them:

> The Grumbling Goblin is a typical tavern with a smokey interior. There are a few folk sitting in small groups here and there, but the place is hardly full. Off to one side and a ways toward the back are a pair of gentlemen seated at a round table. Both of them stand out from the crowd, as they are dressed rather garishly. The first of the two is decked out from head to toe in bright red robes. His companion's outfit, while similar in cut and cloth, is a slightly more subdued gray color. It is a pretty sure bet that they are wizards.

Go through the process of formal introductions. Velinax does most of the talking. Once the characters are seated and a round of drinks have been ordered, read the following to the players:

> The one who calls himself Velinax takes a sip from his drink and then sits back reflectively. "My companion and I," he begins, "are involved in some fascinating research. For a number of years, we have been gathering all sorts of information on beholder lore. It is a wondrous subject. Of course, all of our studies have been abstract in nature—very few people have encountered one of the eye tyrants and come back to tell the tale, much less come back with any useful details.
> "Both of us feel that our studies have gone as far as they can in the laboratory. We are now prepared to do some first-hand field research. We need, however, a little extra muscle to assist us on this mission, because, of course, everyone knows how resistant beholders are to the forces of magic. Therefore, we would like to hire you to join us in our endeavor to gather a normal beholder specimen."

Velinax is more than willing to talk money with the characters once he has made his proposition. Not only will he let the PCs keep all the treasure that they find in the lair, but he will also pay for any expenses that they might incur. If the characters seem reluctant to accept this offer, Velinax

Beginning the Adventure

will offer to pay each character 10 gold pieces a day. He will go as high as 50 gold pieces a day and throw in a star sapphire worth 4,000 gold pieces once the beholder specimen is in his hands. If the characters still seem reluctant, Velinax will hand a bag of gold coins to the character that has shown the most leadership to this point. Inside are 100 gold pieces. This is Velinax's very earnest "gesture of good will."

At this point, the characters must decide if they wish to accept the wizards' proposition, but the rest of the adventure depends on the PCs acceptance of the job. As soon as the PCs agree, read the following aloud to the players:

> Velinax leans back and smiles eagerly. "Wonderful," he says. "Tarren and I are thrilled. Now we can get down to the details. We have reason to believe that a beholder has set up a lair near the logging village of Burke's Crossing. We have already acquired a room at the inn there and begun preliminary investigations. We believe we know where the lair is, so the only thing left to do is explore it.
>
> "We have some additional business to take care of before we return to Burke's Crossing, so what we would like to have you do is meet us at the inn there in two days. The name of the place is the Knotty Pine. That will give you time to take care of anything else you need to before we begin. Agreed?"

There is really little else to take care of at this point. If the characters do not want to split up from the two wizards, the wizards politely explain that the business they wish to tend to is private and refuse to say anything else. If the PCs insist, then you must figure out some way for the wizards to convince the characters to go their own way for the the time being. If the characters try to follow the wizards, then they use magical resources to escape the PCs. If there is just no way for the wizards to avoid the characters, then have Velinax confront them, expressing severe disappointment that there cannot be more trust between business partners. If the characters do

not back down after that, then Velinax tells them that all deals are off and that he will have nothing further to do with them. Once he gets them alone, he may just take his full ire out on them in elder orb form.

If the characters express doubts about their own abilities to face a beholder, Velinax and Tarren assure them that their extensive knowledge will lend the group the edge it needs to defeat the monster. Velinax also hints at a few tricks up his sleeve, but does not wish to give away all of his trade secrets before it becomes necessary. Tarren does speak if spoken to, and he is friendly enough, but he tends to let Velinax do most of the talking, preferring to sit back and observe.

Allow the characters to gather any additional equipment and other supplies they wish to before they set off. The trip to Burke's Crossing takes the better part of two days on foot and two full days by river. If you wish to throw a minor encounter or two at the PCs while they are on their way, feel free. Otherwise, proceed to Burke's Crossing once they arrive there.

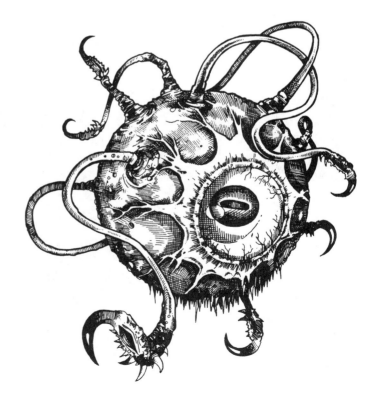

Burke's Crossing

The community of Burke's Crossing grew as a result of the logging industry in the region. It's actually little more than a handful of homes and a business or two in the middle of nowhere. The first real evidence of civilization was Elastis Burke's lumber mill. He set up shop on the bank of the Gambis River, near a shallow ford where the road from Cumbert crosses. Most of the timber that is cut further upstream is processed into building material here and then shipped to Cumbert by either wagons or barges. After the lumber mill was established, a fur trader came, and soon after that the inn was built.

Most of the folk who live in Burke's Crossing are nice, if a little rustic in their attitudes. All of the strange activity has gotten them spooked, but they are hardy folk who figure that whatever problems exist will sort themselves out soon enough. In the meantime, they just go about the business of living. The logging camp itself is nothing more than a clearing with a chow wagon where the loggers eat during the day while they are cutting timber and camp out at night if they don't want to make the long journey home. Most of them have families in and around Burke's Crossing. Of course, there are very few of them who are willing to work at all right now, since they think the woods are haunted.

Read the following aloud to the players when the characters first arrive in Burke's Crossing:

> The journey has been a pleasant one, and not overly long, but it is still a welcome sight when the road crests the next hill to reveal a shallow ford and a cluster of buildings huddled together in the twilight beyond. This must be Burke's Crossing. To the left of the ford is a lumber mill with a huge waterwheel jutting out from its side and revolving slowly in the river's lazy current. Just a little way beyond, a stand of houses clump around a central building. Hanging over the front entrance to this place swings a sign showing a burly woodsman with an axe at his side.

Key Sites

Refer to the area map for a layout of Burke's Crossing, as well as its location in relation to the logging camp and Cumbert.

Burke's Crossing

The Lumber Mill

The lumber mill operates on hydraulic power, using a waterwheel that is connected via fly-wheels and gears to a great bandsaw in the interior of the building. Timber that is floated down from upstream is processed into boards of various sizes inside the mill. There is a shallow man-made inlet next to the building that serves as a holding pen for the logs when they arrive. After the lumber is processed, it is loaded onto wagons and barges and sent to Cumbert or other towns where building supplies are in demand.

The current owner of the lumber mill is Jadon Burke, Elastis's grandson. He runs the business much as his grandfather and father did, although these mysterious events have hurt his profits a great deal. Since the loggers refuse to work, he cannot get timber to make into lumber, and his business is suffering greatly. If something isn't done soon, he may go completely bankrupt.

The Fur Trader

The fur trader, Tholas Dramon, recognized the site of Burke's Crossing as a natural transportation center in the middle of the wilderness, and since the lumber mill was already established, he knew that it would be an easy matter to convince the wagon and barge owners to load his goods, as well. While his son Loric built the building where the business would be run, Tholas began trapping the animals for the furs. There was an abundance of wildlife, so business has been fairly good. The only problem has been the expansion of the logging industry into some of his trapping sites. With the removal of the trees, Tholas's game is migrating further away, making his daily treks to his trap sites longer and longer.

During the last few weeks, Tholas has continued to trap, even though he has been warned repeatedly by his neighbors that the woods are haunted and he'll disappear like all the others. He doesn't buy into any of that nonsense and ignores it. The truth of the matter is that Tholas has been lucky; since his traps are fairly far away from the logging camp, he isn't around the areas Qeqtoxii roams.

The Knotty Pine

Once the lumber mill and the fur trader had set up shop, other people began to see the value of the site next to the ford, and several loggers built permanent homes in the vicinity. After that, a need for other small businesses became evident, and hence the Knotty Pine inn and tavern was established. Tamerick Beyl, the owner of the Knotty Pine, is the widow of an old logger who moved his wife and daughter here when the logging industry first began to boom. Tamerick's husband died from a fall out of the top of a tree he was trimming in preparation for cutting.

When the Beyl family lost their source of income, the enterprising Tamerick decided to try her hand at running an inn. Since many of the loggers in the area had been friends and associates of Tamerick's husband, they devoted time to help her construct the place. In return, she promised them a fine taproom and outstanding fare. They have not been disappointed. Kaywen, Tamerick's daughter, tends the bar while Tamerick herself runs the kitchen. No one bothers the two women, for there's always a dozen or so beefy loggers in the taproom who watch over them like family.

Tamerick offers a simple menu, but her cooking is outstanding. Courses include venison pies, squirrel stew, fresh trout, and other hearty meals fit for a proper woodsman, along with cheeses, fresh bread, cold milk, fresh fruit, and all manner of ales, wines, and meads. The main room is a rough-hewn affair with a huge flagstone fireplace in the middle of one wall. Everything in the place is rough-cut timbers and furs. Somewhat surprisingly, the customers are not all that rowdy; it is probably due to a combination of respect for Tamerick and exhaustion from a hard day's work.

Upstairs, Tamerick has rooms available for rent on either a nightly or monthly basis. She has two loggers who are regular boarders, and the rest of her clientele are folks passing through to somewhere else. She was understandably surprised, then, when Velinax and Tarren took a room at her inn for a month's time. Finally, there is a large barn behind the inn where travelers can leave their mounts, but they must do so at their own risk—there are no stable boys to tend to the horses.

Burke's Crossing

Events

Once the characters are in town, they are likely to go straight to the inn to seek the two wizards, Velinax and Tarren. Thus begins the series of events that should eventually lead the characters to make their way to the lair of the beholder. Listed below are a whole series of events that you can spring on the players. There is no general order to the use of these, except for the first one, which should happen at the outset of this section. Beyond that, use as few or as many as you deem necessary, or until the players get the idea that they should head off to the logging camp to do additional investigating.

Missing Wizards

It is natural to assume that the characters will visit the Knotty Pine right away, seeking Velinax and Tarren. Read the following aloud to the players once their characters enter the inn for the first time:

> The front doors part to reveal a cozy taproom with a large fireplace to one side. The delicious smells of roasting meat and freshly baked pies mingle with the odors of tabacco smoke and pine needles. Perhaps half a dozen men and half as many women sit at various tables, drinking and chuckling amongst themselves. Several of them glance up at your entrance, but they do not give you a second look.
>
> A young woman, fair of face, begins moving toward you with a smile. "Good evening, and welcome to the Knotty Pine. Is it a meal or a room you seek this evening?"

This is, of course, Kaywen. She does not know anything about the two wizards, claiming that her mother Tamerick takes care of all the lodging arrangements with the guests and offering to fetch her for the group. In the meantime, she suggests a hot meal for the travelers, explaining that the menu this evening includes roasted rabbit, cheese, and blackberry pie.

Tamerick will enter from the kitchen shortly after Kaywen leaves with the group's dinner and drink orders. She is an older version of Kaywen, also fair of face, but the lines of many years' work do show. She comes right up to the PCs' table. Read the following aloud to the players, making adjustments as necessary:

> "Evening. I'm Tamerick, the owner. My daughter says you're looking for two wizards. Both of them dressed kind of oddly, one of them all in red? Yes, they were here just yesterday, but departed again early this morning. They gave me something to deliver to some folks that fit your description, though. I'll get it." She heads back into the kitchen, then returns to your table a moment later with a piece of folded parchment in her hand.
>
> "Here you go. This is what they told me to deliver. You look like the travelers they described, and since you're asking about them, I figure you must be the right ones. If there's anything else you need, just holler at Kaywen, and one of us'll make sure you're taken care of." With that, she departs for the kitchens once again.

Once the characters unfold and read the parchment, read the following aloud to the players:

> "Greetings. We trust your journey was pleasant and uneventful. As we are not expecting you until late in the day, we have decided to do some further investigating in the logging camp farther upriver. We shall return by dusk. Let's plan to set out at first light tomorrow. Both of us are eager to get started. Your business partners, Velinax the Vermilion and Tarren Traskar"

If the characters ask Tamerick where the logging camp is, she can explain to them that there is a footpath that follows the river that will take them there. If they ask her any other questions about where the two wizards are, all she can tell them is that they were carrying quite a bit in the way of supplies, but she didn't pay that much attention; she will claim that she does not stick her nose too much into other folks' business.

Burke's Crossing

If the PCs ask right off the bat to be allowed into the wizards' room, she will curtly refuse their request. If they get rooms of their own, however, and spend at least one night there in an obvious attempt to wait for the pair of wizards to return, Tamerick will agree to escort them up to the room for a supervised visit. While she doesn't mind if they poke around a little bit, she will frown on the characters taking anything from the room.

If the PCs do decide to stay at the Knotty Pine, they can have a very tasty meal and sleep in beds that are quite comfortable.

Talking to the Woodsmen

The men and women who spend their evenings in the common room of the inn are friendly and even invite talkative characters to a game of cards, but they know nothing more than Tamerick about Velinax and Tarren.

The place is actually less crowded than usual. Since most of the loggers refuse to work, many of them have chosen to take a quick vacation and travel downriver to a larger community for supplies, a night on the town, or even to permanently relocate.

If the woodsfolk are questioned about any unusual events that have occurred lately, they can tell the PCs about the unusual disappearances that have been taking place recently, but none of them have heard anything about a beholder, and in fact don't even know what one is. Read the following aloud to the players if they bring up this subject:

One of the tavern patrons sitting across the table sits back in his chair and looks thoughtful. "Well," he begins, "there have been some awful strange goings-on around here lately. The woods are haunted, you know—folks keep disappearing."

"Oh, nonsense, Grom," pipes up a woman, appearing as though she hasn't bathed in about two weeks. "Something strange is going on in those woods, but I don't believe in ghosts. Whatever it is, the truth will show itself soon enough."

If the characters ask the woodsmen to elaborate, read the following to the players:

The one named Grom takes a long pull from his mug. "Well, there have been a whole rash of disappearings lately. Several of our other lumberjacks have headed off into the woods to start cutting one morning, and they never came back. No one has seen hide nor hair of them, and when we send out search parties to look for them, there's no trail or anything."

The unwashed woman leans forward and continues. "Yeah, first there was Halvey Kith, then Brial Nermuss, and then Tiny. . . ."

"Each of them disappeared without a trace," says Grom. "I still say it's ghosts. Tiny could have tracked anything, at least anything natural, but the trail always just ends. No footprints, no drag marks, no nothing. And there's never any blood or torn clothes, like a bear'd gotten them or something."

"Tell 'em about the statue," a second man interrupts.

"Oh, yeah, the statue," says Grom, looking thoughtful. "The other day, several folks found a big statue, plain as day, sitting right on a pedestal in the middle of a clearing. Just a bust of some man, nobody knows who. Then, just after sunset, I saw some lights twinkling in the trees near it. They just danced around, all purples and greens, flittin' this way and that. I took off then, and I ain't goin' back. Not for a while, anyhow. If that ain't spooks, I don't know what is."

The woodsmen are willing to talk and speculate the rest of the night about what might be happening, but they have no other hard and fast facts about the situation.

The Rivals Arrive

At some point while the characters are in Burke's Crossing, a second group of adventurers arrive, seeking a woman they claim was to meet them at the Knotty Pine and lead them on an expedition to the lair of a beholder. Introduce this event at some point when the characters are at the inn. Read the following aloud to the players:

Burke's Crossing

The doors to the inn swing wide and in stroll several hardened-looking individuals. From their garb and equipment, it is likely that they are adventurers. The first one in, a woman wearing ring mail and a sword, eyes the place for a moment, taking in the entire scene, before her gaze settles on your table. Her mouth forms a frown, but she doesn't otherwise react. Her three companions—a dwarf with a huge double-bladed axe and a man and woman dressed almost identically in black, tight-fitting clothing—fan to either side of her, also surveying the occupants of the inn.

Kaywen strides toward them with her customary smile. "Greetings, travelers. What may our establishment offer you?"

"We seek a lady knight," replies the armored woman, "A woman who calls herself Mikanda. We were instructed to meet her here. Where is she, wench?"

The smile leaves Kaywen's face as several of the patrons in the room turn in their chairs at this curt remark. "She has a room here," answers Kaywen politely, but without the warmth of before, "but she has not been here in almost a week."

"Very well, then," responds the warrior woman, "Bring us ales, and be quick about it. We want that table over there." The woman begins moving toward a table in the far corner of the room, her companions following, as Kaywen spins on her heel and returns to the bar, her

is a wizardess. The two have been inseparable adventuring companions since childhood. They like to dress similarly, both to establish their relationship and to disguise their skills.

These adventurers do not seem at all interested in fraternizing with the other patrons of the inn, choosing instead to huddle in their corner and wait. If any of the characters approach them, they are unfriendly and unwilling to impart much information. If the PCs reveal that they are here to hunt a beholder, read the following aloud to the players:

At this revelation, the four adventurers become visibly agitated. "I see," says the woman in armor. "Well, it looks like we've got some competition going, then. That's why we're here, too."

The dwarf smacks his hand on the table, causing his mug to jump. "Thunder!" he roars. "We don't need a bunch of juveniles pretending to be heroes going up there and stirring up trouble before we even get started. That'll just make the dang thing mad. Go on back home and leave the beast to us, kids."

"Yes, stay out of our way," threatens Jelifer. "I mean it. You'll just get yourselves, and us, killed."

Jelifer and the others are not interested in making further conversation after that. It should be clear to the PCs that they have competition for this excursion. The NPCs are absolutely not interested in teaming up, since they want to keep the treasure shares as rich as possible. They spend perhaps one more hour in the corner drinking, and then they decide to rent a room for the night and disappear until the next morning. They are up with the following dawn, packing their equipment and heading out to find the beholder's lair.

If the characters think to ask Tamerick, she can tell them that Jelifer and the others left early that morning, before the PCs were awake. She can also mention that they had packed quite a bit of equipment for their journey and had mentioned something about the logging camp. Otherwise, she doesn't know anything more about their intentions.

This rude group of individuals is an adventuring party also hired by Qeqtoxii to infiltrate the lair. However, the elder orb made contact with them in the guise of a female knight, a cavalier seeking retribution for the death of several of her companions. Again, Qeqtoxii has set up an elaborate story to convince the NPC party that the situation is genuine. He even rented "Mikanda" a room at the Knotty Pine for the month to leave a trail to follow.

The NPCs are not evil, just haughty and self-important. The leader of the group is Jelifer Kasma, a warrior. Her companions include Khulgrim Irontoe, a dwarf axeman, and Eris and Londra Camahan, brother and sister. Eris is a rogue and Londra

In the Wizards' Room

At some point the characters are likely to want to investigate Velinax's and Tarren's room. Whether they gain permission from Tamerick or break in themselves, there is quite a bit of useful information to be had. When they first enter the room, read the following aloud to the players:

> The room rented by the two wizards is neat and orderly. In addition to the two beds along opposite walls, there are a pair of trunks at the foot of each bed, a small writing table with some papers neatly stacked on it, and a small armoire in one corner.

The papers on the table contain a variety of information. There is a record of expenses that lists the cost of this room, the costs of having notices printed up in Cumbert, some minor laboratory equipment, and other miscellaneous expenditures. There is a small stack of about four pieces of parchment that have some notes scrawled on them in a messy handwriting concerning the finer points of an anti-magic ray's effects, all very esoteric and of no real use to any-

one but a mage. If there is a wizard in the PC party, explain that the information is complicated and will take weeks to decipher, but that it may definitely be useful some day.

Also among the stacks of papers is a letter from Tarren to Velinax, dated about six weeks previous and in a remarkably different handwriting, describing several new discoveries he has made in recent weeks concerning methods by which beholders levitate. It describes in great detail how Tarren believes that the function is a biological one rather than a magical one. Beyond this, though, the discussion is very scientific in nature. If you also have a copy of *I, Tyrant,* you can refer to that work for more details on what the letter might contain. The letter closes with an urgent plea for Velinax to join Tarren at Cumbert to begin preparations for their expedition.

The footlockers contain nothing more than personal effects, including additional clothing, maps of the area, and so forth. One of the footlockers has a set of bright red clothing, much like Velinax has been wearing, and the other has some similar gray clothing. The footlocker that is Velinax's also contains a book that recounts some lively tales, but the bookmark is a folded piece of parchment. If the

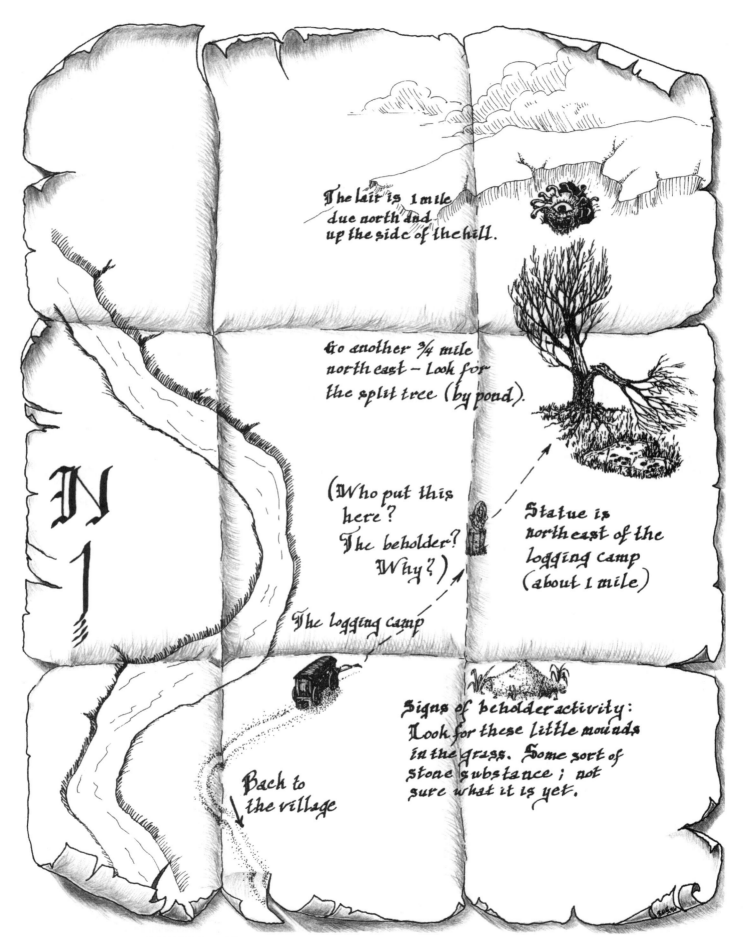

The lair is 1 mile due north and up the side of the hill.

Go another ¾ mile north east – Look for the split tree (by pond).

(Who put this here? The beholder? Why?)

N

Statue is north east of the logging camp (about 1 mile)

The logging camp

Signs of beholder activity: Look for these little mounds in the grass. Some sort of stone substance; not sure what it is yet.

Back to the village

Burke's Crossing

characters think to unfold this and look at it, show them the map and notes on page 14. It is the clearest indication yet of where the beholder lair is. It also contains some notes about ways to track a beholder.

The armoire is empty except for an old robe hanging inside. In one pocket of the robe is a slip of paper with the message, "See Tobrias about the statue. He knows its true value." This is nothing more than a garment that was accidentally left behind by a previous occupant of the room, a merchant who dealt in objects of fine art, and the message has nothing to do with anything going on in Burke's Crossing. It is merely a red herring to sidetrack the characters. While there is no one in either Burke's Crossing or Cumbert named Tobrias, the lumberjacks could inform the PCs that one of their co-workers was named Tobian. If the PCs follow this up, they will discover that Tobian left for parts unknown before the statue ever showed up.

Shadowy Forms

On perhaps the second or third night after the characters have arrived in Burke's Crossing, spring this event upon them. It should take place well into the evening, after dark, while one or more of the characters is outside. Choose or select at random a PC. Read the following aloud to that player:

> Out of the corner of your eye, you detect a hint of movement. Glancing over in that direction, you barely catch the shadowy form of someone sneaking around the corner of the inn.

Give the player the opportunity to have the character follow. If he or she does so, continue reading the following:

> You move to the corner of the building and peer around, but there is no sign of anyone. You are pretty certain that if someone was hiding there, you would be able to see him because the moon is rather bright tonight, and the shadows are rather pale.

The character has spotted a member of a secretive organization that is missing one of its members, a thief named Wilbon. Wilbon's last known whereabouts were right here in Burke's Crossing, but he has not been heard from in several weeks. The organization has sent out a search party to find their comrade, but they do not like to attract attention to themselves, so they tend to skulk around and hide in shadows alot.

This criminal organization is devoted to gathering all types of information on a variety of subjects—primarily for selling, ransoming, and blackmailing. One of its tenets is that it keeps close tabs on its members through a variety of magical means, so if one gets into trouble, others can come to his or her rescue. In this particular case, Wilbon is the unfortunate fellow who Qeqtoxii turned into a statue (see page 20 for more details on this statue). Due to the nature of his eventual destruction, the organization has been having trouble locating him. They are now skulking around in Burke's Crossing, trying to find out who knows what.

There is no game reason for these guys to be here, other than the possibility of throwing a red herring at the characters. Their appearance is left open-ended for you to follow up on later, should you desire. If you are running this adventure as part of a greater campaign, then this could easily be a thieving guild or other criminal organization that is already established. If none of those fit, or if this is an isolated adventure scenario, feel free to flesh out this organization however you wish. It will undoubtedly utilize a combination of thieves and wizards in its work, using clever combinations of stealth and magic to hide and sneak. For example, the members of this team might utilize a *rope trick* spell to avoid detection out in the woods.

One of the possible side effects of this event is the mistaken assumption on the players' parts that the mysterious figure in the darkness is one of the NPC adventurers. If they come to this conclusion, let them believe it. It will be even more convincing later if you also run The Explosion.

A Moonlight Tryst

This is another good event to run while the characters are outside late at night, especially if they are getting jumpy. Kaywen, Tamerick's daughter and the barkeep at the Knotty Pine, has been seeing one of the younger and more handsome of the loggers. Although she is certainly old enough to be courted, she is afraid her mother will disapprove, so she and Cordell have been sneaking out into the woods late at night for some moonlit rendezvous.

While one or more of the characters are out in the woods, read the following aloud to the player(s):

> Sounds in the woods always seem to distort at night, and this evening is no exception. The nighttime sounds of a hooting owl, a croaking tree frog, and other nocturnal critters scurrying through the underbrush seem to bounce and shuffle among the pines, making it difficult to tell exactly where things are. The moon is bright, however, and the evening seems peaceful.

> But wait! Was that a shadow moving up ahead? There is the sound of a large branch snapping, and then something drifts slowly between two trees in the dim distance. Even in the bright moonlight, it is impossible to tell what it was, but it was certainly big.

If the characters choose to use stealth to follow the shadow, lead them on a nice goosechase for several minutes. Have them lose the trail only to spot the form once again as it reappears up ahead. If they decide to charge forward and attack immediately, they run into a clearing and find themselves face to face with Cordell, who has raised his axe to defend himself and is panicked. He makes an attack at the first character to appear before he realizes who they are. Otherwise, the PCs can eventually sneak up on the romantic couple in a small clearing, sitting side by side on a log, holding hands and talking softly. The appearance of the characters in this case certainly frightens the pair, but Cordell does not automatically attack this time, giving the PCs a chance to identify themselves. When the mistaken identity is exposed, the lovers are deeply embarrassed that

Burke's Crossing

they have caused so much trouble, but also because they have been found out.

If the characters accidentally kill one or both of the trysters, the mood in Burke's Crossing will become somber and less friendly toward the PCs. While they will not openly blame the characters for the tragedy (after all, it was pretty foolish for the two lovers to go sneaking out into the very woods that have been the source of so much trouble already), the folks of the community, particularly Tamerick, will disapprove of the characters' overzealous approach to solving this mystery and will want nothing more than for the characters to leave.

Break-Ins

This is another red-herring episode. The members of the criminal organization continue to search for Wilbon. They have begun to break into several citizen's houses while those people are away, searching for clues to the whereabouts of the missing thief. They are not actually taking anything, merely pawing through all of the folks' belongings, searching for items that might have been taken from Wilbon's body.

The trespassers leave few clues behind. Remember, they can use magic to avoid leaving the usual tell tale signs. The characters can attempt to follow up on these activities and try to locate the criminals, but if the PCs turn up the heat too much on them, they most likely will bolt, returning once things have quieted down. As an alternative reaction to character pressure, see the next event.

The Explosion

WARNING: This is a potentially deadly event; be certain your characters can survive it before using it in the game. This event works well as a retaliation for the PCs' nosiness in the criminal organization's activities. One evening, when the PCs return to their room to retire for the night, read the following aloud:

> You open the door to your room only to catch a glimpse of a shadowy figure exiting through the open window. When you race to the opening and look out, the intruder is nowhere to be found.

Allow the characters to determine a course of action. Whatever they decide, the figure has snuck off (perhaps with the aid of a *teleport* spell). The PCs will very likely go through all of their belongings to see if anything was stolen. Nothing has been taken.

In actuality, the intruder has planted a magical *time bomb* in their room, up on an overhead beam (the ceiling of the characters' room is slanted, like the roof, and there are some support beams running where a flat ceiling would normally be). The *time bomb* has been set to go off 20 minutes after the PCs enter the room. This should give them enough time to run back downstairs to try to catch the intruder and then return to get ready for bed.

Allow the most observant character in the group to roll a saving throw vs. spell (alternatively, you can require a proficiency check against an alertness trait or something similar, if you use those rules). If the check succeeds, the PC notices the *time bomb,* which looks like an hourglass with sand draining from top to bottom. Otherwise, no one notices the item *unless a player specifically states that his or her character is searching the room top to bottom or looks up at the ceiling.* When all the sand empties from the top of the hour glass, the bomb explodes, inflicting 5d6 points of damage to everyone within a 20-foot radius (essentially, everyone in the room). This explosion is identical to a *fireball* spell, so a successful saving throw vs. spell reduces the damage by half.

If the *time bomb* is spotted before it detonates, it can be disarmed by tipping it over or shattering it. Once this happens, the magic is forever negated. It could still function as a normal hourglass if it was not damaged, however. For more information on this magical item, see the *Tome of Magic.*

The Final Lure

This final event can be run in one of two ways; either in or around Burke's Crossing (assuming the characters hang around there for quite a while and do not get around to traveling to the logging camp), or once the characters begin to search for the lair of the beholder.

As a final lure to the characters, Qeqtoxii, in its beholder form, has cast a *veil* spell (modified for beholders) that fools the PCs into thinking that Tarren is a beholder. There is one reason for this act: to remove Tarren from the picture. Qeqtoxii wishes to work freely from this point on, so it has put Tarren into a situation that will most likely be deadly for the hapless wizard.

When Tarren comes floating out of the trees towards the PCs, they are likely to think that he is the beholder they have been tracking and attack him. By the time Tarren figures out a way to convey his message to the characters, it is too late to prevent any fast-reacting PCs from attacking. Unfortunately for Qeqtoxii, the elder orb's spell on Tarren wears off before he can be destroyed by the PCs.

Read the following aloud to the players when you are ready to run this event:

> Just through a stand of trees, movement catches the corner of your eye. You turn to look and spot some sort of bulky form. You're not certain what it might be, but it is big.

Give the characters a chance to react. If they move to get a better view, read the following:

> Closing the distance between yourself and the silent mass that you have detected through the trees, you begin to get a clearer view. A few more strides, and it will be within sight. Whatever it is, it is moving through a clearing just beyond a final stand of trees and underbrush.
>
> When you finally get a good look, your pulse quickens; a great sphere, a good five feet in diameter, drifts slowly toward you. A large central eye stares unblinking right in your direction, while 10 more eyes atop stalks ringing the creature's head glance this way and that distractedly. A fierce gaping maw is open, saliva pooling and dripping from the partially protruding tongue. The beast seems to have spotted you and is coming right at you.

This should make it obvious to the characters that they face a beholder. Of course, they don't know that it is actually Tarren, so play up the shock value and vicious appearance of the creature as much as possible. If for some reason they don't close the distance to see what's going on in the woods, Tarren moves toward them, wanting to get their attention, but not calling out to them. (He doesn't want to draw the beholder to his location.) In this case, read the following aloud to the players when Tarren breaks into the clearing:

> A great sphere, a good five feet in diameter, passes through the underbrush, breaking into the clearing. A great central eye stares unblinkingly right at you while 10 more eyes atop stalks ringing the creature's head glance this way and that distractedly. A fierce gaping maw is open, saliva pooling and dripping from the partially protruding tongue. The beast seems to have spotted you and is coming right at you.

In his eager rush to meet the characters after seeing a beholder nearby, Tarren runs to the characters with the intention of imploring them to help him. Unfortunately, he is heedless of the image he is creating and the danger he is putting himself in by charging the characters.

Whether the characters go into the woods, or Tarren is forced to emerge from them, play the scene up as an attack as much as possible without actually having Tarren do anything violent or

The Final Lure

even call out. The whole idea here is to convince the characters that this truly is a beholder so that they will attack.

If the players for some reason decide not to slay the beholder, then the *veil* spell wears off just about the time that they decide something is not right and cease their attacks. Tarren returns to his natural human form right before their eyes. He begins explaining everything that has happened to him that day.

Basically, after Tarren and Velinax left the group in Cumbert, they teleported to Burke's Crossing. After getting some gear together, the two of them set out to look around the lair. Nothing much came of their scouting, so the two of them left the area to take care of some other nonrelated business. Unfortunately, this business took a little longer than Velinax had anticipated. Once they were done, Velinax dropped Tarren back off at the clearing containing the statue so that Tarren could study it further before walking back to town to meet the PCs. That's when Tarren saw the beholder.

If the players were clever enough to figure out that something wasn't quite right with this scene and didn't slay the wizard, then kudos to them. They deserve the rewards of saving Tarren's life. Grant each character 500 experience points as a bonus for clever thinking. Tarren will be an invaluable addition to their party, should they wish to include him in their escapades.

In the event that the characters slay Tarren in beholder guise, then the following scene should occur as the killing blow is struck. Read the following aloud to the players when this happens:

> This last attack is a telling blow, knocking the beholder backward in a gout of blood. The creature shrieks in pain from the obviously mortal wound. It settles to the ground slowly, spasming in some sort of death throes. Then, something truly remarkable happens. Before your very eyes, the spherical mass of the beholder's body begins to change shape by shrinking, lengthening, and taking on another form entirely.
>
> The gray of the beholder's body becomes the gray of cloth; eye stalks disappear and are placed by arms and legs. The face of the beast contorts and becomes human. When the transformation is complete, a human lies before you, bleeding and obviously dying. It is a human you know well, however. It is the wizard Tarren. He stares at you wild-eyed, confusion mingled with fright. He seems to want to tell you something.

The characters will most likely want to take actions at this point. Allow them the opportunity to heal the mage. Once he seems to be in stable condition, he will inform the characters of the current situation.

If the PCs are unable to help Tarren, he will be able to pass on a few short sentences about a beholder before dying. If they search his body, they find his spellbook, a note about the physical characteristics of a death tyrant, his *ring of blinking*, and several assorted coins in a small pouch: 14 cp, 9 sp, 3 ep, 5 gp.

The Logging Camp

Eventually, the characters should head toward the logging camp to track down the location of the beholder lair. Consult the map to see the footpath that leads from Burke's Crossing to the logging camp. When the characters first enter the large clearing where the logging camp is located, read the following aloud to the players:

The well-worn trail has followed the small river for perhaps four miles when it finally breaks into a great clearing. In the middle of the place sits a large chuckwagon, although from the way the wheels have settled into the earth, it isn't likely that the wagon has moved in a long time, since it seems to have sunk into mud during a rain shower or two.

At first, no one seems to be about, but then, you detect some activity coming from the far side of the wagon, out of sight. At the next moment, a grizzled old man strolls into view, carrying a huge pot in both hands. He spots you standing there and nods, but doesn't change his direction to come meet you. He moves toward the river.

This is Dak, the cook. He is fetching water to begin the noon meal for the lumberjacks, although there are very few still willing to work at present. If the PCs move to talk to him, read the following aloud:

The grizzled fellow acknowledges your introduction with a crooked smile and another nod. "Name's Dak." He doesn't break stride as he mentions this, continuing to chop vegetables, start a fire, and skin a brace of squirrels. "I heard of you folks. Everyone says you're looking for those two wizards. Can't say that I've seen them. But I've seen your friends."

He's referring to the NPC party. They passed by on their way to the lair. Dak admits that the last time he saw them was the morning they departed the Knotty Pine (you will have to determine how many days have passed for the characters since then). Dak doesn't know much else, but he can point the way to the strange statue. He offers the characters lunch if they are interested in sticking around long enough. "There's more than enough," he says. "What with most of the loggers refusing to work, I'm having a hard time avoiding wasting food."

The Mysterious Statue

In a clearing not far from the logging camp but higher into the hills, a statue has been created and erected by Qeqtoxii. Read the following to the players the first time the characters enter this clearing and spot the statue:

In the middle of a perfectly circular clearing, a slender stone column stands, perfectly smooth and about three feet in height. Atop this pillar sits the bust of a man, flawlessly sculpted. Every feature is finely worked, down to the pores in the skin. A true craftsman had to have created this piece of art. The figure itself has long, wavy hair that hangs to the shoulders, a beard and moustache, and a scar beneath the left eye. It wears an expression of confusion mixed with a touch of terror.

This is the petrified form of Wilbon the traveler, a rogue caught in the wrong place at the wrong time. Qeqtoxii encountered Wilbon during an evening "stroll" near Burke's Crossing. The elder orb immediately petrified the man using its *flesh to stone* eye power, then began carving portions of Wilbon's body and limbs away through careful use of its *disintegrate* eye power. Once it had a proper bust remaining, it used the *telekinesis* eye power to whisk the "statue" back to its lair.

On a whim, Qeqtoxii decided to scare the

locals with its creation, so it set about carving from a large boulder a pedestal that it could use to display the bust. It moved this into the clearing near the logging camp and set it upright, again using its *telekinesis* power, then transported the bust in a similar manner to the site and placed it atop the pedestal.

It is possible to remove the bust from the pedestal, but it weighs about 70 pounds. If it is dropped, the bust must make a saving throw vs. crushing blow (use the thick wood category) or have its nose chipped off.

If the PCs spend any time looking around the area, they easily notice quite a few small stone projections jutting up from the ground. They look almost like miniature stalagmites. They are in actuality the petrified remains of beholder droppings left behind by Qeqtoxii as further evidence of his own presence. (The waste material of a beholder is left behind as little piles that harden to the consistency of rock after a short time. For more information on this, refer to *I, Tyrant*.)

Clever players may pick up on this evidence, remembering the notes on the wizards' map about piles such as these (see page 14). If they think of it, they can follow the waste piles to the lair, which is not too far from this site. Qeqtoxii has actually left an overabundance of the things, trying to make it easier for the characters to find its secret hideout. By this time, smart players may begin to realize that they are being almost inundated with clues, and they may begin to think that they are being manipulated. Obviously, you don't want to spoil the fun by giving this fact away, but consider rewarding such intelligent thinking with an experience-point bonus.

The Lair

Finally, the characters have reached the object of their long and convoluted search. Whether they have arrived here by following a map, tracking the petrified waste heaps left by Qeqtoxii, or even being led by Tarren, they have come to the heart of the adventure. The characters have reached the spot marked as The Lair on the players' map.

The mouth of the cave can be found high upon a ledge and is not easily spotted from the flatter ground below. In addition, it has been carefully covered over with brush to disguise it further. Explain to players who have been following the trail of miniature stalagmites that those markers end here. For those characters who are using the map, tell the players that this seems to be the area described in detail on that map. Once the characters begin searching for further clues as to the exact location of the entrance, roll secretly for each character to detect a concealed door. Once a successful roll is made, read the following aloud to the players:

> A few dozen yards up the side of a steep hill there is a long ridge with an outcropping of rock that serves as a shelf. At one point along this ridge, the back wall of the hillside is recessed. Shrubs grow thickly, but it appears that there might be a deeper niche hidden behind them.

Characters can attempt to ascend the hillside unaided, but each must roll a successful Dexterity check or slip on loose gravel, trip over a tree root, or in some other way lose their footing and tumble back downward, suffering 1d4 points of damage in the process. If, however, the characters are cautious and utilize rope tied to the trees to work their way up the hillside, no Dexterity check is necessary.

If Tarren is still with the party, he makes it known to the PCs that he wishes to stay outside the lair. Read the following aloud:

> Before you can attempt to scale the hill, Tarren clears his throat in an attempt to get your attention. "I regret having to say this, my friends, but I feel that I would only hinder your efforts inside that cave. I have been a research mage all of my life and my spellbook tends to reflect that. I have learned a few spells that might prove to be useful, but only after the beholder is taken care of." Tarren pauses for a moment before going on. "Of the two of us, Velinax is the one that should be going with you. If you will allow me to, I will wait for him outside the cave."

Tarren truly feels that he would hinder the party's efforts once inside the cave. He doesn't have any spells that will help anyone but himself, but he will go inside if forced to. However, he makes a point about his knowledge of the *stone to flesh* spell. Tarren points out that if he is the one that suffers from the beholder's *flesh to stone* ability, he won't do the party any good whatsoever.

Once they are at the top, it is obvious to the members of the party that trimmed brush has been laid across a cave mouth to camouflage it. The hidden entrance is round and approximately six feet in diameter. It leads back into the hillside at a steep angle for approximately 60 feet to Area 1.

Any characters attempting to descend through this tunnel run the risk of slipping on some loose gravel about halfway down. Have each character make a Dexterity check at one-third their score to avoid this *unless they are taking some kind of precaution to prevent it, like tying rope to an anchor and holding onto it.* Any character that fails this modified ability check slips and falls and begins sliding down the tunnel. (Note: Any light sources that the character is holding may be extinguished. Assess a chance and roll to see if this happens.) The character must now roll a saving throw vs. spell; success means that the PC has managed to halt the downward movement. Failure means the character is sliding down the tunnel and building up speed.

The Lair

The sliding PC will crash into any characters that are farther down the tunnel (that is, in front of the character in line), possibly knocking them down as well. The character immediately in front of the sliding PC must roll a saving throw vs. spell to avoid being knocked down, too. If *that* roll fails, both characters begin sliding, possibly knocking down *another* character in front of them. For each additional sliding character that collides with a standing character, a –4 penalty is added to the saving throw score for the upright PC to remain standing.

As soon as a PC successfully avoids being knocked down, all the characters stop sliding and may stand and continue down the tunnel to Area 1. If sliding characters do not manage to stop themselves, they reach Area 1 and fall over the edge of the ledge to the rocky floor of the cavern. Each suffers 2d6 points of damage and is subject to attacks from the creatures there.

Area 1

Read the following aloud to the players *only* if their characters arrive on the ledge under their own power; do not read this to players whose characters have slid down the tunnel and fallen over the ledge:

> The steep tunnel descends for a few dozen yards and opens onto a narrow ledge near the top of a very large cavern. There is a distinct smell of dampness and decay here. Stalagmites and stalactites are in abundance, creating a columned room with an uneven, rocky floor about twenty feet below the level of the ledge. It is impossible to tell how large the cavern is; its far walls are hidden in darkness beyond the limits of your light source.

If the PCs ask about using a stalagmite or something to secure a rope, mention that a sturdy stalagmite has formed on the ledge. Any rope that is secured to this particular formation will provide the PCs with a safe way to descend to the cavern floor.

For this room, Qeqtoxii has cultivated several special denizens to serve as a deterrent to other species entering the cave system. There is a whole nest of shriekers here, along with a single violet fungi and a handful of boring beetles. They are unable to get out since the two exits are so high off the floor of the cavern.

Of course, Qeqtoxii simply drifts through this area without disturbing the creatures, floating high enough above the floor of the cavern that they never notice the elder orb come and go. The characters, on the other hand, will most likely cross this area on foot, agitating the shriekers and thus attracting the attention of the boring beetles. Anyone who moves more than 15 feet away from the base of the ledge alerts the shriekers, who immediately begin their customary screeching. One round later, the boring beetles scramble into view and move in to attack.

Shrieker (Fungus) (5): AC 7; MV 1; HD 3; hp 18, 11, 10, 7, 7; THAC0 17; #AT 0; Dmg nil; SD noise; SZ M (4'–7'); ML steady (12); Int non (0); AL N; XP 120 ea.

Notes: Light within 30 feet or movement within 10 feet causes a shrieker to emit a piercing shriek that lasts for 1d3 rounds.

Violet (Fungus): AC 7; MV 1; HD 3; hp 13; THAC0 17; #AT 3; Dmg see below; SA rots flesh; SZ M (6'); ML steady (12); Int non (0); AL N; XP 175.

Notes: The violet fungus is able to make three attacks with its three 2-foot-long branches. These branches excrete a substance that rots flesh in one round unless a successful saving throw vs. poison is rolled or a *cure disease* spell is used.

Boring Beetle (Beetle, Giant) (9): AC 3; MV 6; HD 5; hp 26, 25 (×2), 24, 21, 20, 18, 16, 15; THAC0 15; #AT 1; Dmg 5d4; SZ L (9' long); ML elite (14); Int animal (1); AL N; XP 175 ea.

Occasionally Qeqtoxii will "freeze" its little nest of creatures in order to sort through whatever they have managed to scavenge off their victims, looking for treasure. Since this is such a remote location, the elder orb has found very little, but most of what it does have is stored away deeper in the lair. Of course, in an effort to

The Lair

help prepare the characters for their further obstacles, Qeqtoxii has left a few "presents" for the party. These include a slightly lopsided *ring of cantrips,* a scroll containing the spells *feather fall* and *stone to flesh,* a *quarterstaff +2,* a jar of *Keoghtam's ointment* and a *ring of feather falling.* They have to spend some time searching for all of the items, but for every ten minutes spent searching, allow the party to find another item. As for money, the PCs have the possibility of gaining one pearl worth 250 gp and some coinage equalling 16 gp, 7 ep, 23 sp, and 15 cp.

The opposite side of the cavern also has a tunnel exiting from it higher up along the wall. At first, this tunnel is natural in form, just like the rest of the area the PCs have passed through so far. About 25 feet into it, though, the tunnel suddenly becomes smooth and perfectly round, obviously worked and shaped artificially. The elder orb has done this to appeal to its own sense of aesthetics. This tunnel leads another 20 feet into a great circular room, Area 2. Once again, the PCs can rope a sturdy stalagmite that has formed on the ledge and make their way up the wall.

Area 2

Read the following aloud:

> The worked tunnel you have been following opens into a similarly wrought area that appears to be perfectly round. The floor, ceiling, and wall are all perfectly smooth—obviously artificially created. The diameter of the place is perhaps 30 feet across, and the ceiling is 15 feet above the floor. In the very center of this chamber is a six-foot-diameter shaft in the floor. The rest of the place is utterly devoid of decoration of any kind.

The shaft leads downward to Area 3. It has been carved and worked so finely that its surfaces are utterly sheer. It is treated as a completely smooth wall, so even thief characters cannot descend this surface without the aid of rope or tools. The shaft drops for about 200 feet before reaching the bottom, noted below as Area 3. However, at the spots marked Area 2a through Area 2d on the map, there are traps.

At these four locations, there are very small holes in the walls of the shaft that connect to a parallel shaft that is reached from Area 5. Xaxinaar, the death tyrant that Qeqtoxii created, can float and peer through these holes in the wall, making attacks with its eye powers at intruders as they descend the shaft. There are a variety of attacks possible depending on the circumstances (that is, the method the characters are using to descend the shaft). These are mixed up to keep the characters guessing.

If the PCs are using rope to descend, Xaxinaar waits at the top hole until all the characters are below its position, then it uses its *disintegration* power on the rope. Alternatively, it will disintegrate the rope at the *lowest* location, preventing the PCs from completely descending, and then use its *flesh to stone* power on the highest character, causing that PC to petrify on the line and begin sliding down the rope, colliding with the PCs below and knocking them down. All the characters will be forced to fall, as the petrified PC is much too heavy for another character to support.

The exception to this is if some holds have been worked into the rope—loops or knots—that can be used to support the PCs' weight. In this instance, the petrified character does not slide down, but it does block the lower characters from climbing back up easily. Xaxinaar then begins picking them off one by one with its *cause serious wounds* eye power.

If the characters use a magical means of descending the shaft (such as a *feather fall* or *levitate* spell), Xaxinaar simply uses the *anti-magic ray* of its central eye to cause the spell to vanish. Xaxinaar sometimes uses more direct attacks, including *flesh to stone, cause serious wounds,* and *sleep.* The chance of a character noticing any of the small holes in the wall of the shaft is slim (10%) even in well-lighted conditions unless a player announces that the PC is specifically looking for something like that. If this is the case, then the PC has a 50% chance to notice the small holes.

The Lair

Area 3

The shaft leading down from Area 2 ends in a large open pit that is half-filled with water. Any characters that fall from inside the shaft fall into this water, suffering only half normal falling damage from striking the surface. Of course, characters in heavy armor, or those who do not know how to swim, are still in no small amount of trouble, because the water is 15 feet deep. In addition to this, a giant bloodworm lives in these waters, feeding on those creatures that fall down the shaft.

Giant Bloodworm (Worm): AC 4; MV 6, Br 1; HD 6; hp 28; THAC0 15; #AT 1; Dmg 1d8; SA blood drain; SZ H (20' long); ML fanatic (18); Int non (0); AL N; XP 420.

> Notes: When the bloodworm makes a successful attack, it attaches itself to its victim and continues to drain 1d8 hit points worth of blood each round until removed (requires a successful open doors roll) or killed.

The bloodworm attacks the first creature that falls into the water by pushing itself off the bottom of the pool and wrapping itself around the victim it latches on to. It then pins the victim's appendages down, preventing him from defending himself or swimming. The bloodworm sinks to the bottom of the pool to feed, most likely drowning its victim. It will ignore all other creatures in the pool once it has attached itself to a victim, even if attacked.

Scattered along the bottom of the pool are four gems that Qeqtoxii has never bothered to fetch: one moss agate (10 gp), one black opal (125 gp), and two pieces of smokey quartz (50 gp each).

A perfectly round single tunnel of six feet in diameter leads out of this area at ceiling height. PCs with the ability to climb can enter this tunnel by scaling the slanted wall.

Area 4

The tunnel from the water pit (Area 3) travels for about 60 feet before opening into Area 4. Read the following aloud to the players as their characters approach this area:

> There seems to be some sort of weak, indirect light source of a sickly green color up ahead, apparently coming from a large room beyond this tunnel. As you near the end of the passage, you can see the room. It is round, and the walls glow with the green light. In the middle of the room, a lone figure kneels, head bowed.

Give the players a chance to have their characters take action. The glow comes from a special fungus that is luminescent; Qeqtoxii cultivated it to provide light within the lair. If the PCs begin to enter the room or otherwise make their presence known to the figure in the middle of the place, read the following aloud. If you did not introduce the group of NPCs as one of the events in Burke's Crossing, you must modify the text slightly:

> The figure raises its head upon noticing you. It is Jelifer Kasma, the warrior you met back in Burke's Crossing! "Don't come in here!" she warns you. "You'll become trapped, like me." As she says this, she gestures at her feet, and you can now see that she is not kneeling at all, but rather her legs from the knees down have been literally embedded in the floor, which is made of a rich, black stone.

Jelifer is the victim of *blackstone*, a mysterious magical material that beholders created as a means of protecting their lairs. Any time a beholder passes its *anti-magic ray* gaze over blackstone, it ceases to exist for one round, then appears once again. Anything occupying the same space as the blackstone when it rematerializes becomes encased in the blackstone (without being damaged), and that amount of blackstone disappears forever. For more information on this substance, see *I, Tyrant*.

Qeqtoxii set this room up with the floor actually 1½ feet below the mouth of the entry tunnel and then placed a layer of blackstone over it that was flush with the tunnel. Qeqtoxii's instructions to Xaxinaar regarding Jelifer's group were to float high overhead in the room and wait for victims to walk out on the floor, and then turn its gaze toward the floor for an instant. This caused the blackstone to vanish and then reappear around anyone standing on it, trapping them. This is exactly what happened to Jelifer, and she has been here ever since.

If questioned, Jelifer can tell the characters that she and her companions managed to get this far into the lair (they used Londra's *levitate* spell to get out of the pool of water before the bloodworm got to them), but they were caught by surprise with the floor. All four were trapped, and the beholder petrified the rest of them and then removed them from the area, leaving only her behind. She is exhausted (it's hard to sleep standing up) and very hungry. She doesn't know how to make the stone disappear, but she begs the characters to figure out a way to free her.

Neither Qeqtoxii nor Xaxinaar will appear while the characters are here, preferring to wait and see what the characters do about this situation. Unless they can cast a *dispel magic* or *stone shape* spell or have some stone-working tools that they can use to chisel her out, they cannot free her. When this becomes obvious, she begs them to kill her. Jelifer cannot bring herself to do it herself, so she wants a PC to aid her. It is up to you as DM to decide if a player uses good role-playing to resolve this situation and deserves an experience-point reward.

Area 5

Area 5 is actually a vertical extension of Area 4, a vast space that rises high over the floor of magical blackstone. Again, the walls of this place have been worked perfectly smooth by judicious use of *disintegrate* eye powers, and they are covered with glowing green fungus, so even thieves cannot climb them without tools and ropes. The area actually rises for about 160 feet. About two-thirds of the way up, there are several small ledges. Resting on these ledges are the statues forms of Khulgrim, Eris, and Londra, Jelifer's three companions.

The ledges upon which the NPC characters are embedded within are made of blackstone. This means that if attempts are made to restore them to flesh through the use of a *dispel magic* spell (which won't work for that particular purpose), the blackstone will disappear for one round. Anything on the shelf (including the NPC) immediately falls as the shelf ceases to exist.

It is this stage of the lair that Qeqtoxii considers to be the beginning of the actual living quarters; this wide vertical shaft resembles an entry parlor. The elder orb used the petrified invaders

as decorations, but also as bait to lure unwitting PCs into casting the *dispel magic* without the proper preparations and causing themselves or the statues to fall.

Area 6

Area 6 is the main gallery of the lair where Qeqtoxii has done most of the decorating. Read the following aloud to the players when their characters reach the end of the short tunnel leading from Area 5 to Area 6:

> The small round hallway widens at this point, and the place is surprisingly well lit. Ornamental gems embedded in the alcove walls emit brilliant magical light. The worked stone here includes intricate patterns that have been carved into the floor and walls. To either side of the way are alcoves with statues set into them. The craftsmanship of the whole gallery is exquisite.

The statues are actually missing citizens of Burke's Crossing, petrified and brought here to decorate the hall. They are all intact, and if the characters can rescue them and get them returned home, an experience-point reward is in order. You as DM must decide what is appropriate, considering the particulars of your campaign.

The ornamental gems are actually set into a kind of pattern in each alcove. The brightest light comes from the 36 ornamental gems placed in each alcove (216 gems worth about 5 sp each). The light from these gems serves to highlight the statues with various colors. There are also three semiprecious stones in each alcove that provide a softer, similar-colored light behind the statue (total of 18 gems worth 50 gp each). Then, directly behind the head of each statue is a precious stone that pulsates softly (total of 6 gems worth 100 gp each). These gems are nothing more than decoration. If a character wishes to pry them from the wall, it will take a round of prying plus a successful Strength check before the gem will pop free of the wall.

IMPORTANT NOTE!: Xaxinaar is hiding in Area 7, using his *anti-magic ray* eye power to negate the existence of a wall of blackstone that is indicated by the dotted line on the lair maps. Once all the characters pass beyond this point into Area 7, Xaxinaar releases the *anti-magic ray*, and the wall reforms, trapping the characters. They cannot retreat back into Area 6. While Xaxinaar is maintaining the ray, however, any magic ceases functioning within its line of sight, so keep this in mind while the characters are in the special shaded area on the map. Any spell effects cease, and no new spells can be cast here.

Area 7

In this area, the final confrontation with Xaxinaar takes place. By this time Qeqtoxii has already skipped out through a rear exit (see map), leaving the death tyrant behind to destroy or be destroyed by the PCs. Area 7 of the lair actually resembles an arena; it consists of the main circular room (again with very smooth, unclimbable walls) surrounded by a raised "walkway" around the perimeter with a low balustrade to offer some cover.

Read the following aloud to the players when their characters enter this area and become trapped by the reappearance of the wall of blackstone:

> Beyond the hall of statues lies a large circular room with a high ceiling. It is more dimly lit than the previous area, but there is some sort of overhead balcony running around the perimeter of the room. There do not appear to be any exits from this place other than the one through which you entered. Even as you make a note of this, however, the light grows suddenly dimmer, and you realize that where a passageway existed before, now a sheet of that mysterious black stone is forming in the missing portion of the rounded wall. You are trapped in here!

The idea here is that the characters enter this room from Area 6, and then Xaxinaar releases the *anti-magic ray* eye power so that the wall of blackstone blocks their retreat. At that point, the death tyrant begins attacking the characters, using the balustrade as partial cover. To make matters more interesting, there is also a collection of gas spores here. One of the first things Xaxinaar was ordered to do is to use *telekinesis* to move gas spores up over the top of the balustrade and down into the pit to interfere with characters' actions and possibly force them to accidentally attack the spores. While the characters are distracted with the gas spores, Xaxinaar utilizes other eye powers to attack the PCs (except for *anti-magic ray*—Qeqtoxii ordered the death tyrant to hold off on that so that the wall of blackstone would not be affected and the characters could not escape).

Once the death tyrant has come forward to battle the PCs, be sure to describe its middle eye as being covered with a milky film. Also, throughout the battle, it would be a good idea to reference Xaxinaar's unusable eyestalks and even the moss that seems to be encrusting him. In other words, hint to the PCs that they are facing a death tyrant without *saying* "you are facing a death tyrant." Hopefully, one of the PCs will mention the beholder's strange traits to Tarren, if the mage isn't present to identify the nasty creature in person.

Gas Spore (Fungus) (4): AC 9; MV 3; HD 1 hp; THAC0 20; #AT 1; Dmg special; SA special; SD special; SZ M (4'–6' dia.); ML average (8); Int non (0); AL N; XP 120 each.

Notes: When struck, a gas spore explodes, inflicting 6d6 points of damage to all within 20 feet (saving throw vs. wands for half damage). If a gas spore comes into contact with exposed flesh, it shoots tiny rhizomes into the living matter and grows through the organism within 1 round. The gas spore then dies immediately. The victim must have a *cure disease* spell cast upon him or her within 24 hours or die, sprouting 2d4 gas spores. Beholders are immune to all the effects of gas spores.

Xaxinaar (Death Tyrant, Undead Beholder): AC 0/2/7; MV Fl 2 (C); hp 47; THAC0 11; #AT 1; Dmg 2d4; SA eye powers; SD immunity to *sleep, charm,* and *hold* spells; SZ L (5' diameter); ML fanatic (18); Int nil (except for comprehension of orders); AL LE; XP 13,000.

Notes: *Eye Powers:* central—*anti-magic ray* (140-yard range, 90-degree arc before beholder; no magic functions in that area), plus the following eye powers: 1st—variant *hold monster;* 2nd—*sleep* (as spell, but only one target); 3rd—*telekinesis* (250-lb. weight); 4th—*flesh to stone* (as spell, 30-yard range); 5th—*disintegrate* (20-yard range); 6th—*fear* (as wand); 7th—*slow* (as spell, but only a single target); 8th—*cause serious wounds* (50-yard range); 9th and 10th eye stalks no longer function.

Qeqtoxii created this particular death tyrant from the corpse of a slain companion within Ixathinon's hive. The creature's name was Xaxinaar, but of course it has no memories of its life. Qeqtoxii has given Xaxinaar a complex set of instructions regarding defense of the lair. There are set procedures for each step of the characters' penetration into the various areas, and Xaxinaar obeys them fully and completely

Wrapping Up

As was mentioned previously, there is a bolt hole that Qeqtoxii uses to escape the lair before the characters can catch him. A tunnel leads out of Area 7 and to a very long vertical shaft straight up; again, this is so smooth that not even thieves can climb it unaided. At the top, it exits out at the top of the hill where the PCs first discovered the entrance to the lair. If the PCs ever decided to check out the hill, then it is possible for them to spot this exit, but only with a successful concealed door roll made secretly by the DM. By the time the characters manage to escape the lair, the elder orb is long gone, taking most of his treasure with him in his *bag of holding*. However, if the PCs search the arena's balcony after destroying the death tyrant, they will find a few scattered gems and precious stones (one violet crystal garnet worth 500 gp, a golden yellow topaz worth 450 gp, and three aquamarines worth 500 gp each), several coins (35 cp, 42 sp, 6 ep, and 36 gp), a wizard scroll containing the spells *dispel magic* and *polymorph self*, a *potion of extra-healing*, two jars of *Keoghtom's ointment*, a *dart of the hornet's nest*, a *long sword +2*, a *hammer +2*, a set of *elven chain mail* that will fit an elf or half-elf, and a small bag of *Puchezma's powder of edible objects*.

If you are planning on continuing this plot with the next adventure in the series, *Eye of Pain*, then the following event occurs when the characters return to The Knotty Pine in Burke's Crossing. Read the following aloud to the players when this happens:

> As you enter the Knotty Pine, tired and wounded, Tamerick the owner rushes up to you excitedly. "Your friend was just here," she exclaims excitedly. "He said that he was heading for Cumbert and didn't have time to wait for you. He told me to tell you to meet him back at the Grumbling Goblin when you make it back here. He just cleaned out his room, settled his tab, and left not very long ago at all."

When the characters ask Tamerick who she is referring to, she tells them the wizard in the red clothing, Velinax the Vermilion. Qeqtoxii intends to lead the characters on quite a wild goose chase, which begins in *Eye of Doom*.

Award Guidelines

It is ultimately the DM's responsibility to hand out story and group awards to reflect how well the group has role-played, worked together, etc. However, some guidelines have been provided with this adventure that will help DMs in their final estimation of what to award a group in several specific instances (not including the XP earned by destroying monsters). If the party wishes to advance more slowly (such as a group that has five or more adventures per level of advancement), then decrease the awards. If a party wishes to advance more quickly, then increase the awards. Of course, the DM can assign further points if the party does something unique (in other words, not listed here) that forewards the plot.

- In the Wizard's Room: By finding the bookmark map in Velinax's room, the party earns a total of 500 XP.
- The Explosion: If the party disarms the time bomb, then they earn a total of 500 XP.
- The Final Lure: If the party does not attack Tarren when he is disguised as a beholder, then they each earn 500 XP.
- The Mysterious Statue: If the party figures out that they can follow the beholder droppings to the lair (without the help of the map), then they each earn 300 XP. If they figure out that the beholder droppings are planted evidence meant to lure them on, then they each earn 500 XP.
- The Lair: If the party heals the brown bear, then they earn a total of 1,000 XP.
- Entering the Lair: By finding the lair, the party earns a total of 1,000 XP.
- Area 4: If the party helps Jelifer out of her prison, they earn a total of 1,000 XP.
- Areas 5 and 6: If the party manages to restore the statues to life (with the help of Tarren, for example), they earn 1,000 XP per statue restored. Since there are a total of nine complete statues, then it is possible to earn a total of 9,000 XP.

Major NPCs

Here are the entries for all the major NPCs in this adventure. Feel free to modify any of their statistics to suit game balance. Note that any NPCs not listed in this section (such as the citizens of Burke's Crossing) are considered to be 0-level humans.

Qeqtoxii (Elder Orb Beholder): AC 0/2/7; MV Fl 3 (B); hp 75; THAC0 5; #AT 1; Dmg 2d4 (bite); SA eye powers, spells; SD anti-magic ray, immunity to *sleep*, *charm*, and *hold* spells; MR 50%; SZ M (6' diameter); ML fearless (19); Int godlike (23); AL LE; XP 18,000.

Notes: *Eye Powers:* Central—*anti-magic ray* (140-yard range, 90-degree arc before beholder; no magic functions in that area), plus the following eye powers: 1st—*charm person* (as spell); 2nd—*charm monster* (as spell); 3rd—*sleep* (as spell, but only one target); 4th—*telekinesis* (250-lb. weight); 5th—*flesh to stone* (as spell, 30-yard range); 6th—*disintegrate* (20-yard range); 7th—*fear* (as wand); 8th—*slow* (as spell, but only a single target);9th—*cause serious wounds* (50-yard range); 10th—*death ray* (as *death* spell, but single target, 40-yard range).

Spells (Qeqtoxii can only memorize one spell per level at a time): 1st—*feather fall, hold portal†;* 2nd—*darkness 15' radius*, detect invisibility*, ESP*†, knock;* 3rd—*dispel magic*, protection from normal missiles*†;* 4th—*control death tyrant**, dimension door, extension I, instruct spectator**, polymorph self†* (note that polymorphing himself into humanoid form does not allow Qeqtoxii to cast spells with material or somatic components); 5th—*contact other plane, teleport†, wall of blackstone**, wall of force*;* 6th—*extension III†, geas;* 7th—*phase door, power word stun†, teleport without error, vanish, veil;* 8th—*create death tyrant**, mass charm, power word blind†;* 9th—*Mordenkainen's disjunction, power word kill, prismatic sphere†, time stop.*

†Indicates favored memorized spell. *Indicates an elder orb variation on an existing spell—it requires only verbal components, takes twice as long to cast as the normal variety, and is known only to elder orbs. **Indicates a special spell that appears in *I, Tyrant.*

Qeqtoxii is a brilliant and cunning creature, able to plan for almost any contingency and detect and eliminate all flaws in logic in its complex schemes. If it has one shortcoming, it is understanding the nature of human thinking, which isn't always logical at all. Since it has begun interacting with humans, however, it is getting better.

Qeqtoxii craves power above all else. It burns with the desire to overthrow the hive mother it currently serves and take her place. The elder orb insinuated itself into her hive in the guise of a true beholder and bides its time until it can usurp her. Its plans for this are complex and time-consuming, but the elder orb is patient. It has worked for several years to make this a reality.

Qeqtoxii will not allow its enemies to detect and corner it; if it is in danger of direct contact, it will use whatever means it has at its disposal to escape notice, most likely through the use of spells. It is definitely not in the elder orb's best interests to be seen by the PCs yet.

Qeqtoxii has several magical items at its disposal, which it can easily use when necessary. The first of these is a *bag of holding*; it stores all the elder orb's other magical items and important possessions, including its spellbook, in this magical container. Others include potions of *extra-healing, gaseous form, human control* (humans), and *water breathing*; an *amulet of proof against detection and location* (which has been specially crafted to be worn around one of its eyes and which it wears rather than stores); and a *Daern's instant fortress.*

Tarren Traskar, hm, M12: AC 10; MV 12; hp 31; THAC0 17; #AT 1; Dmg 1d6 (quarterstaff); SA spells; SD spells; SZ M (5' 3"); ML average (8); AL LN.
S 12, D 12, C 8, I 15, W 16, Ch 12.
Personality: enthusiastic, quiet.
Special Equipment: ring of blinking, quarterstaff.
Spellbook (4/4/4/4/4/1): 1st—*comprehend languages, detect magic*, detect undead, erase, feather fall*, find familiar, identify;* 2nd—*detect invisibility, ESP*, fool's gold, forget, invisibility*, wizard lock;*

Major NPC's

3rd—*blink, clairaudience*, clairvoyance*, dispel magic*, explosive runes;* 4th—*hallucinatory terrain, illusionary wall, improved invisibility*, Leomund's secure shelter, magic mirror, remove curse;* 5th—*airy water, avoidance, fabricate, sending*, stone shape, transmute rock to mud;* 6th—*enchant an item, legend lore, stone to flesh*, true seeing.*

*Indicates favored spell.

Proficiencies: ancient languages, astrology, dagger, dart, herbalism, navigation, quarterstaff, reading/writing, religion, rope use, speak common, speak regional, spellcraft.

Tarren has always been fascinated by unusual creatures, and beholders are his favorite subject. Unfortunately, this made him all the more susceptible to the proposed alliance between Velinax and himself. When Qeqtoxii realized the full potential of having Tarren as an unwitting ally in his schemes, it wasted no time in convincing the wizard that they should work together. Since that time, Tarren has been the elder orb's pawn, playing associate to the mythical Velinax the Vermilion.

Jelifer Kasma, hf, F6: AC 7 (*ring mail*); MV 12; hp 35; THAC0 15 (14 with specialization); #AT 3/2; Dmg 1d10+3/3d6+3 (two-handed sword with Str bonus and specialization); SZ M (6' 0"); ML champion (15); AL NG.
S 16, D 7, C 11, I 11, W 14, Ch 11.
Personality: brash, focused.
Special Equipment: potion of giant strength, ring mail, bastard sword, heavy crossbow, two-handed sword.
Proficiencies: bastard sword, endurance, heavy crossbow*, hunting, mountaineering, rope use, speak common, speak regional, two-handed sword* (* denotes specialization).

Jelifer is the leader of a group of adventurers who are very mercenary in their approach to life. While not evil by any stretch of the imagination, she is haughty and unfriendly toward those she considers beneath her station, which includes just about everybody who isn't nobility or who haven't proven themselves to be her match in combat. She believes anything can be accomplished if the right people are doing the job, and she and her team are the right people.

No matter what the characters say to Jelifer, she is not about to give them any credit for anything. Only after they have in some way demonstrated their abilities to her first-hand (such as surviving the beholder's lair and perhaps rescuing her and her comrades) will she grudgingly accept them as equals. Until that time, she is not interested in interacting with the PCs.

Khulgrim Irontoe, dm, F5: AC 4 (*brigandine +2*); MV 6; hp 29; THAC0 16 (15 with Str, 13 with *battle axe +2,* 12 with specialization); #AT 3/2; Dmg 1d8+5/1d8+5 (*battle axe +2* with Str bonus and specialization); SD reduced AC (−4) vs. size L creatures; SZ M (3' 11"); ML elite (14); AL LN.
S 17, D 13, C 12, I 7, W 11, Ch 5.
Personality: haughty, sour.
Special Equipment: brigandine +2, battle axe +2, dagger, heavy crossbow.
Proficiencies: battle axe*, heavy crossbow*, mountaineering, navigation, rope use, speak common, speak dwarvish (* denotes specialization).

Khulgrim Irontoe never much liked humans, until he met Jelifer. She showed him that not all humans are either pathetically noble and out to save the world, or heinously evil and trying to rule it, as he had originally feared. Instead, he learned that some humans are just interested in making lots of money, and that suited him just fine. The two of them have been adventuring partners ever since, and he hasn't regretted it yet. While he holds no serious fondness for Jelifer (or the other two humans he travels with, for that matter), he at least knows he can trust her to watch his back, just as he'll watch hers.

Eris Camahan, hm, T4: AC 7 (leather, Dex bonus); MV 9 (lightly encumbered); hp 11; THAC0 19 (20 with Str penalty); #AT 1; Dmg 1d4/1d3 (2 daggers); SA backstab; SD thieving abilities; SW −1 penalty to magical defense adjustment; SZ M (5' 5"); ML unsteady (7); AL CN.
S 7, D 15, C 10, I 10, W 6, Ch 14.
Personality: oily, cowardly.

Major NPC's

Special Equipment: leather armor, 2 daggers, thieves' picks, 50' silk rope, pitons.

Thief Abilities: PP 30, OL 40, F/RT 35, MS 25, HS 25, DN 35, CW 95, RL 15.

Proficiencies: dagger, disguise, juggling, jumping, knife, reading lips, rope use, short sword, tumbling.

Eris Camahan has been traveling with his sister, Londra, since they were kids. When their parents died, they were adopted by their aunt and uncle, who worked in a traveling carnival. That is where Eris and his sister learned their trades. Even as children, they began to sneak off between shows to explore, and soon enough, they left the carnival life behind to see the wider world.

They met Jelifer and Khulgrim in a backwater town in an alley fight with some thugs. Although they defeated the attackers and chased the hoods away, they soon found out that they had crossed a very powerful criminal guild. The four of them fled the city and the prices on their heads, and they have been traveling as a team ever since.

Eris is not much of a fighter, but he can smooth-talk his way out of a jam as often as not. He leaves the grunt work to Jelifer and Khulgrim, figuring that's what they are best suited for. He figures himself as the true brains of the operation, but he's content to let Jelifer think she runs things.

Londra Camahan, hf, Inv4: AC 10; MV 12; hp 17; THAC0 19; #AT 1; Dmg 1d6/1d6 (quarterstaff); SA spells; SD spells; SZ M (5' 9"); ML steady (11); AL NG.

S 10, D 13, C 16, I 13, W 13, Ch 10.

Personality: cool, hard-edged.

Special Equipment: wand of illusion, quarterstaff.

Spellbook (3/2): 1st—*change self, color spray*, dancing lights, Nahal's reckless dweomer, shield*, wall of fog** 2nd—*ESP*, flaming sphere, fool's gold, improved phantasmal force*, knock, Leomund's trap, levitate, magic mouth, web, whispering wind.*

Proficiencies: juggling, navigation, quarterstaff, reading/writing, spellcraft, tumbling.

*Indicates favored spell.

Londra is definitely her brother's sister. She carries herself in the same manner he does, and strangers seldom realize she is a wizard at all, thinking the pair of them are acrobats or whatnot. This suits her just fine, for she has found that the world tends to be more impressed with a woman who looks like she can handle herself in combat than one who can sling a spell or two. Not that she really cares what the world thinks about her, but fewer people bother her this way.

Londra and Eris have always been close, and their personalities show it. They finish each other's sentences regularly and very often they will be able to know what the other is thinking with only a look. When in battle, they act as one, blending into the background and working for a surprise attack on the flanks of the enemy.

Londra tends to be a little bit colder than her brother and a little less willing to strike up a conversation with strangers. While she doesn't find fault with Jelifer or Khulgrim, she doesn't feel particularly interested in becoming close friends with them, either. She simply trusts them to do their jobs, and she has vowed to do hers. If the two warriors ever got unfriendly with the pair, Londra would not hesitate to split the group up by coaxing her brother to seek other adventuring opportunities.